Table Of Contents

Introduction

My history with ADHD, my long path to diagnosis, my decision to accept this diagnosis as part of my identity is the story of how I started to reimagine my life at the age of 20. I was living with the somewhat confused understanding that this confusion was another one of life's hazards: teaching me to manage distraction, to forget things; teaching me to underachieve. And that is the story of what it was like to live as a 20-something with ADHD.

My diagnosis of ADHD crept up on me completely by surprise. In much of my earlier life, my friends, my family, even my teachers assumed that my inability to focus, and my lack of organization and follow-through were due to my inherent 'laziness', or my 'lack of trying'. It had taken a particularly difficult semester my sophomore year of college before I sat down with a university counselor, and after an array of testing, the diagnosis came back. It was the first time I could make sense of what had seemed like a scattered narrative.

Getting diagnosed at 20 was both a relief and a challenge, 'For me, mostly it was a relief because now I knew why I had all these problems, but at the same time, I was also kind of disappointed because it's like, "Oh no, now I have to learn how to deal with this.' My social life, grades at school and even sense of self-worth suffered, but I didn't want to be defined by

ADHD. Instead, I decided to work with it and learn how to manage.

figuring out how to manage ADHD has been an all-encompassing process. Medication helped me immensely with focus and impulsivity, but I knew I couldn't simply rely on meds. So, I came to be adept at time management techniques such as the Pomodoro method. I used planners and set notifications on my phone as reminders. I joined support groups and found camaraderie and relief having a community of peer experiences to compare.

In the decades after my graduation, ADHD also played a role in my professional life. Deadlines, multitasking, and the fast tempo of the work environment seemed daunting. Creating my own open-channel with the powers-that-be in my job, as well as utilizing the skills I'd developed and the coping mechanisms I'd learned, allowed me to create a supportive work environment that has sustained me through years in the profession. With ongoing effort, I was able to achieve professional growth and satisfaction.

Yes, life with ADHD can present real difficulties. Being easily sidetracked, struggling to focus and two steps behind with the latest requests from those around you, all this can be tough. Yet it has been an opportunity to push myself. To find my voice in a world where lacking it is a real barrier to success. To talk about the issues, I need help with and – as my doctor friend, one of the first people to tell me I have ADHD, suggested – to develop a bag of tricks of how to work around difficulties. Getting lost in the process can make it even harder to find the path ahead. In the end, it can provide a map to reach goals.

As a child, I was always thought of as daydreaming, or just not paying attention during class. The consensus from my family, teachers, and friends was that I was lazy, uninterested, or simply not trying hard enough. Not until I was a teenager was I diagnosed with Attention-Deficit/Hyperactivity Disorder (ADHD) and given an answer for why I was having so many difficulties when I was younger. However, a diagnosis didn't make it any easier to live with ADHD.

ADHD symptoms vary from person to person, but my problems with focus were both hyperactive and inattentive in nature, which meant that I was equally inept at sitting still and accomplishing a task and switching to a new project at the expense of the current one in its early stages (I once started painting my living room after only half an hour of planning). The everyday chores of daily life, from cleaning my room to completing homework assignments, were unmanageably long and without end.

Deadlines were onerous burdens, the 9-to-5 a mismatch for my erratic energy rhythms. Yet there was also a considerable dark side to my ADHD. The creative energies of my hyperactive mind – the tendency to jump from idea to idea – made many academic and professional activities feel like stifling chores. A standard workday was a mismatch for my erratic energy rhythms, and deadlines were oppressive burdens. However, my ADHD also brought with it some unexpected benefits. It meant that I approached the world in a distinctive way, as though from a fresh perspective – a look that is often fertile with opportunities and innovation. I discovered that the quicksilver quality of my mind made me natural at occupations featuring lateral thinking. I gravitated towards roles that required thinking on my feet and undiluted creativity and was eternally grateful to my 'neurodiverse' mind that helped me stand out from the norm.

Perhaps harder than any of the organizational challenges I face in my day-to-day life is the way ADHD enjoyed a social stigma for a long time: I bear the weight of the belief that my diagnosis is a way of excusing laziness and a shortcoming in discipline, a misapprehension that, to some extent, added pressure to an already burdensome endeavor. 'Don't disclose it,' I said, half-chuckling. 'Work twice as hard, do twice as well, do twice as much, expect it – for the things that you know others can do without having to consciously keep track, even if just mentally, of 10 different things.'

ADHD management is a formidable but multifaceted endeavor that usually combines medication and therapy. For me, it involved a combination of stimulant medication, cognitive-behavioral therapy (CBT), and mindfulness and meditation practices that helped me pay attention, reduce my activity level, and cope with distractions that I might otherwise find too overwhelming.

Relationships were another area where ADHD played up as I found it hard to stop interrupting or losing track of time and conversations or simply forgetting to pick up the phone, even though I'd made a date to call. 'Sometimes I needed to call if I didn't want to continue the relationship,' I remember. I learned to be open and honest from the start, to talk about my ADHD and how it affected my life. My loved ones, when I was honest, became more able to understand and support me. The next time someone says to you: 'Oh, he must have ASD,' remember all the things you don't know about that person or the disability that you are seeing.

Even so, I can't deny that living with ADHD is tough – still, it's in no way deprived of its rewards. As my case shows, it is very much possible to live a full and productive life, with the support of family and colleagues helping people like me see day-by-day that there's no need to feel bad about their talents or potential. If the people around them just harnessed a little more understanding and empathy, the ADHD stigma would naturally, gradually, start to dissipate.

RECOGNIZING YOURSELF Note which of these traits affect your day-to-day life, so you can reflect on them as we proceed in this book: **FORGETFUL**: Do you forget what people have told you? Do you forget where you put things? Do you need reminders for every day things? Do you miss appointments? **ACHIEVING BELOW POTENTIAL:** Do you feel you underachieve for how well you can do in your life? Do you feel you should be getting better grades than you do at school, or should have made it further than you have in your career? **STUCK IN A RUT**: Are you having a hard time moving ahead in your life? Do you feel like you're trapped trying to keep your head above water, playing catch-up instead of living how you want to? Are you stuck in important areas of your life, such as at work or in school?

TIME CHALLENGED: Are you often late? Do you often underestimate the amount of time that things take? Does time drift away? Do you have trouble figuring out how long a task is "supposed" to take?

MOTIVATIONALLY CHALLENGED: Are you a procrastinator? Do you do things at the last minute or need the pressure of a deadline to get things done? Do you have a hard time getting started on tasks? Do you get partway done with many tasks but have trouble completing them?

IMPULSIVE: Do you do things without anticipating consequences (making decisions, shopping, driving, sex, drugs)? Do you blurt things out in conversation? Do you engage in risky sexual behavior? Do you make purchases without considering the cost or your budget?

NOVELTY SEEKING: Are you often bored? Do you seek out new, stimulating experiences to avert boredom? Do you say yes to new obligations when you are already too busy?

DISTRACTIBLE: Do sights, sounds, thoughts, or lower-priority activities distract you from what you should be doing? Do you find yourself daydreaming on a daily basis?

SCATTERED

: Are things messy in your personal space? Is there chaos on your desk, in your house, or in your car? Is it hard to stay on top of what you need to do, and when you need to do it?

Chapter 1: Understanding ADHD in Adults

What is ADHD and how does it manifest in adults?

Let's take a closer look at the ADHD MINDS traits.

FORGETFUL: Forgetfulness disrupts life in many ways, from leaving things behind at home, to failing to make an important phone call, to neglecting important e-mails. Someone we know thought his car had been stolen until the police had found it in a commuter lot – and only afterwards did he completely recall that. he had ridden the train the day it "went missing."

ACHIEVING BELOW POTENTIAL: "Could've done better," "Not working up to potential," or "Makes too many careless mistakes": This is the It was a kind of feedback adults with ADHD often heard as kids and continue to hear now. about themselves now. They, and the people in their lives—parents, teachers, bosses, spouses, and friends—feel they have underperformed and missed out on opportunities that should have helped   them   thrive.
STUCK IN A RUT: For people with ADHD, feeling stuck is not just mild and temporary; it is a life pattern.

ADHD MINDS traits drain energy and increase the effort that it takes to succeed at school or work or to achieve other personal goals.

It's about feeling stuck doing work you're just not good at; stuck doing a job that's not a good fit; stuck trying to get a job you want, while you watch others get the ones they want; stuck feeling undervalued or underappreciated; stuck dealing with difficult colleagues or managers. These are the environmental hazards of modern work, the barriers and dysfunctions that make doing your job harder than it needs to be. But not all stuckness is bad. If anything, stuckness is a basic condition of being human. We train, work, organize and design our tools to avoid certain kinds of stuckness – but we know perfectly well that it's impossible to completely eliminate. Stuckness is essentially a natural state of body-mind dyssynchrony. school, not knowing where you are headed and underachieving; stuck in your parents' basement, still financially dependent on them. This sense of imprisonment leads to a pervasive feeling of being demoralized and losing hope for what could be a bright future.

TIME CHALLENGED: Many people with ADHD underestimate the length of time that things last. They don't really keep track of time when doing something that stimulates them, leading to chronic lateness and rushing through and hope things will be sorted out at the last minute.

They often don't have a sense of just how much 'should' be. accomplished in a day, so they never know whether they've done enough. **MOTIVATIONALLY CHALLENGED**: Most people procrastinate on chores like paying bills, cleaning the loo or going to the gym. On the other hand, George and Yasmin are deeply involved with school politics and had plans to become teachers, but found themselves unhappy and occasionally in tears, questioning why they had chosen that career path if their desire and intention to change to make a difference was so strong. (Perhaps they turn off his phone service so that he can afford ADHD medication). the bills; the clutter makes it hard to find everyday items; the gym membership is left unstarted for many years. There are lots of things, apart from difficult things, that it is hard to get started on. —it seems nearly impossible. **IMPULSIVE**: Impulsivity has many faces.

It's being verbally impulsive, cutting people off in conversation; it's spending money you don't have; it's constantly changing your mind and making decisions without anticipating Consequences; why you're doing things, what's behind you doing it, why you're jumping into your job or quitting your job.It's weird, because the next day, you could be the happiest you'll ever be.

form of bingeing on alcohol, drugs, or food, or driving carelessly. Even a little bit of impulsivity in an adult's life can have significant consequences. **NOVELTY SEEKING**: The trait of novelty seeking is about craving the new. Being unable to manage boredom, the mind always jumps to the next "shiny" thing. This can make it extremely difficult to complete tasks. Obligations pile up that can't be fulfilled. Sometimes even sticking with a relationship can be a challenge. Boredom is also a toxic state because of what people do to avert boredom—oversleeping, overeating, spending hours playing video games, losing themselves on Facebook or YouTube instead of getting work done. For some, novelty seeking and poor impulse control are an entry to drugs, alcohol, or other high-risk activities that can ruin lives. **DISTRACTIBLE**: Distractibility may be the most common of all the FAST MINDS traits. Many people with ADHD have trouble paying attention.

They may stare for hours at something that particularly interests him or her, yet cannot pay attention in any ordinary sense of the term. have not been able to dwell on for more than a minute or two to other things.' Yet they could fill their heads with ever more of this gossip. with so many different thoughts simultaneously that it is impossible to follow just one.

The sensations of the normal run of things make it useless to work in normal darkness of city life. a busy office or study anywhere without complete silence. **SCATTERED**: People with ADHD can be disorganized, though not all are. Like James, their cars and living spaces can be filled with clutter—becoming tripping hazards, fire hazards, and relationship hazards. Scattered people finish work on projects down to virtually the last minute, or even later. And their minds jump from one topic to another. to the next, making accomplishments and conversations a challenge.

WHAT CAUSES ADHD?

It used to be thought that ADHD was a kids-only problem. Just give them they will, with time, grow out of it.We now know that, give or take, 4 per cent of them will, in the end. adults meet the criteria for ADHD.2 We aren't sure exactly what causes ADHD, though scientists believe it's a combination of genes and environment. Many insults disrupt the exquisitely choreographed development of the brain, such as lead poisoning or smoking during pregnancy.

Although demands of modern life put a premium on focused, sitting work, international studies suggest that the frequency of ADHD in children is not much different between more and less developed regions of the world 3 There is little support for the notion that television or media or modern life causes ADHD, though present-day demands to perform and unlimited distractions on the Internet can highlight people's limitations. But technology also offers new opportunities for adapting, with online calendars and downloadable tools. We describe ways of using many of these resources in the second section of the book. ADHD is often carried in the genes. Twin studies are a classic method for determining whether a condition is inherited or due to experiences—and they provide powerful evidence that it's a genetic condition. In more than 75 per cent of identical twins, if one has ADHD, the other is likely to as well.

On the other hand, ADHD is present in only about half of identical twins in which only one child has the disorder.

But what about fraternal twins, who share only about 50 percent of their genes? The fact that nearly three of four fraternal twins of someone who has ADHD also have it indicates that environmental factors, not just genetics, must play a role in the disease.

However, that still leaves open the question of what other factors are involved. Fleur Watson is a student in the classics department at University College London who has struggled with ADHD her entire life. She stood out in class, was easily bored, and found it hard to pay attention. At home, she was impulsive and a little rough around the edges, skipping over amusingly unfortunate circumstances. She did fairly well in school, but this took a lot of effort. Had she been born later in that same class, she might have received a diagnosis of ADHD. On the other hand, in rural Australia where Walker practises, ADHD is not formally diagnosed. Instead, children who fit the profile are taught behavioural strategies to help harness their energy. So it's more a matter of labelling than anything else. Both GP Dr Ned Walker and Dr Bulti making ADHD one of the most strongly inherited conditions in mental health.4 If you've got parents with ADHD, a decent chance you'll have ADHD too.5. So, much of what causes ADHD is hard-wired.

There are clear brain differences, visible with brain-scanning techniques that compare tiny differences in structure and real-time pictures of what the brain is doing during mental activities. We come back to these in later chapters.

Attention and hyperactivity get top billing in the formal diagnosis of ADHD; they emphasize problems controlling attention and overactivity. But up to half of adults with ADHD may also have differences in brain capacities for other "executive functions"—the "boss" capacities of the brain.6 These include the shifting one's priorities, planning, paying attention to the time of day, and ceasing an activity and starting another. As we explore in later chapters, these biological differences contribute strongly to the organizational struggles, the difficulty forming habits, and the unhealthy daily styles of life mentioned earlier. In the section that follows, we identify both these patterns and the specific supports needed to limit their effects. In our experience, medication is a cornerstone in the treatment of ADHD. Medication often makes it easier to control focus and behavior, but it takes adopting new habits and applying strategies for a person to thrive.

Volumes of research show that medication works by increasing levels of neurotransmitters already present in the brain. But other science, including Dr.

Surman's work with his colleagues at Massachusetts General Hospital, part of Harvard Medical School, shows that a combination of awareness, useful strategies, and effective support can transform the struggle of ADHD into a life well lived. There are plenty of successful people with ADHD in many fields: actors and singers, such as Howie Mandel, Adam Levine;[7] sports stars, such as swimmer Michael Phelps,[8] hockey player Cammi Granato,[9] and quarterback Terry Bradshaw;[10] and business leaders such as JetBlue Airways founder David Neeleman[11] and Kinko's founder Paul Orfalea.[12] A painter we know says her ADHD behaviors boost her creativity in the studio. Having FAST MINDS traits can mean there is a mismatch between the way how the brain works and how life demands you to function. It is a way of thinking and being. renders you less competent in today's world. This book endeavours to make thatoss. journey easier.

ADHD, or Attention Deficit Hyperactivity Disorder, is a neurodevelopmental disorder that affects both children and adults. While it is often associated with childhood, many individuals continue to struggle with

ADHD symptoms well into adulthood. In adults, ADHD can manifest in a variety of ways, including difficulty focusing, impulsivity, hyperactivity, and poor time management skills. These symptoms can have a significant impact on daily life, making it challenging to succeed in work, relationships, and other aspects of life. It is important for individuals with ADHD to seek proper diagnosis and treatment, as managing the symptoms can greatly improve quality of life and overall well-being. Therapy, medication, and lifestyle changes are common approaches to managing ADHD, and with the right support, individuals can learn to navigate their symptoms and thrive in their personal and professional lives.

One of the key characteristics of ADHD in adults is difficulty with organization and time management. This can manifest in various ways, including trouble keeping track of deadlines, appointments, and responsibilities. As a result, individuals with ADHD may often feel overwhelmed and stressed due to the constant struggle to stay on top of their tasks. Additionally, they may find it challenging to prioritize tasks and follow through with projects, which can ultimately hinder their ability to reach their goals and succeed in both their personal and professional lives.
It is not uncommon for adults with ADHD to also struggle with maintaining routines, managing finances, and staying focused on long-term goals. This can lead to feelings of frustration, self-doubt,

and a sense of being constantly behind in various aspects of life. Seeking support from healthcare professionals, therapists, and support groups can be beneficial in developing coping strategies and improving overall quality of life for individuals with ADHD.Another common manifestation of ADHD in adults is impulsivity.

Adults with ADHD may struggle to control their impulses, leading to impulsive decision-making, risk-taking behavior, and difficulty regulating emotions.

This can contribute to challenges in relationships and work environments, as impulsivity can lead to conflict and misunderstandings with others. Impulsivity can also manifest in impulsive spending, difficulty maintaining focus on tasks, and a tendency to interrupt others during conversations. It is important for adults with ADHD to seek support and strategies to manage their impulsivity to improve their relationships and overall functioning in various areas of their lives. In addition to difficulty with organization and impulsivity, adults with ADHD may also experience challenges with focus and attention. They may have trouble staying on task, following conversations, and completing projects that require sustained attention. This can make it difficult to excel in work settings that require focus and concentration, leading to feelings of underachievement and frustration.

Additionally, individuals with ADHD may struggle with time management, memory, and maintaining relationships due to their symptoms.

These difficulties can impact their overall quality of life and self-esteem, making it important to seek out support and strategies for managing their ADHD effectively.

Overall, ADHD can manifest in a variety of ways in adults, impacting their ability to succeed in various areas of life. However, with the right support and strategies, adults with ADHD can learn to manage their symptoms and thrive. By understanding the nature of their ADHD and developing coping mechanisms, individuals can unlock their potential and achieve their goals, leading to a more fulfilling and successful life. Seeking therapy, medication, and support groups can also be beneficial in managing ADHD symptoms and improving overall well-being.

Common misconceptions about ADHD in adults

As adults with ADHD, it is crucial for us to acknowledge and confront the prevalent misunderstandings surrounding this condition. One of the most pervasive misconceptions is the belief that ADHD is a childhood disorder that disappears as individuals grow older. Yet, extensive research has demonstrated that ADHD can and does persist into adulthood, exerting its influence on multiple facets of daily life including professional productivity, personal relationships, and overall quality of life. Another misconception is that ADHD is simply a lack of discipline or willpower. In reality, ADHD is a neurodevelopmental disorder that affects the brain's executive functions, such as attention, organization, and impulse control. Individuals with ADHD often struggle with these functions, making it difficult for them to stay focused, prioritize tasks, and manage time effectively.

Unfortunately, the misconception that ADHD is simply an excuse for laziness or incompetence persists among many individuals. This damaging stereotype often results in adults with ADHD feeling ashamed and guilty, deterring them from seeking the necessary help and support. It is crucial to recognize that ADHD is a valid medical condition that necessitates accurate diagnosis and effective treatment in order to empower individuals to excel in various aspects of their lives. Some individuals may believe that medication is the only effective treatment for ADHD, but it's important to recognize that there are a variety of options available. While medication can certainly help manage symptoms, it's not the sole solution. Therapy, coaching, and lifestyle changes can also play a significant role in effectively managing ADHD symptoms and enhancing overall well-being.

It is absolutely essential for adults diagnosed with Attention Deficit Hyperactivity Disorder (ADHD) to dedicate sufficient time and effort towards exploring a diverse range of treatment options available to them. By thoroughly examining and experimenting with different strategies, individuals can better pinpoint the most effective methods for effectively managing and alleviating their symptoms.

Embracing a holistic approach to treatment not only empowers individuals to navigate the challenges associated with ADHD with greater ease, but also significantly contributes to overall improvements in their well-being, satisfaction, and quality of life. In conclusion, it's vital for adults with ADHD to challenge common misconceptions surrounding the condition and seek support and understanding from others. By educating themselves and those around them about ADHD, individuals can become empowered advocates for their own needs and thrive in all aspects of their lives.

Remember, you're not alone in your ADHD journey, and there are numerous resources available to help you unlock your full potential and lead a fulfilling life.

The impact of ADHD on daily life

Living with ADHD can have a significant impact on daily life for adults. From struggling to stay organized and focused at work to dealing with impulsivity and forgetfulness in personal relationships, the challenges of ADHD can be overwhelming. It's important to recognize how ADHD affects various aspects of your life, including time management, communication, and emotional regulation. By acknowledging these challenges, you can begin to explore different strategies and techniques to effectively manage symptoms and ultimately thrive in all areas of your life.

One of the most common ways that ADHD impacts daily life is through difficulties with time management and organization. Adults with ADHD may find it challenging to prioritize tasks, meet deadlines, and keep track of appointments. This can lead to feelings of frustration and overwhelm, as well as negative feedback from others who may perceive them as unreliable or disorganized.

Developing systems and routines to help stay on top of responsibilities can be crucial for managing these challenges.

Another way that ADHD can impact daily life is through struggles with impulsivity and emotional regulation. Adults with ADHD may have difficulty controlling their impulses, leading to impulsive decision-making and behavior that can have negative consequences. Additionally, emotional

regulation can be challenging, with mood swings and difficulty managing stress and frustration. Learning coping strategies such as mindfulness, deep breathing, and cognitive behavioral therapy can help regulate emotions and reduce impulsivity. It is important for individuals with ADHD to seek support from mental health professionals and develop a personalized treatment plan that addresses both impulsivity and emotional regulation.

By implementing these strategies consistently and seeking ongoing support, individuals with ADHD can improve their daily functioning and overall quality of life. Maintaining relationships can also be challenging for adults with ADHD. Forgetfulness, distractibility, and difficulty listening can strain personal and professional relationships.

Communication is key in managing these challenges, as well as setting boundaries and expectations with others. Seeking therapy or couples counseling can also be beneficial in improving communication and understanding in relationships affected by ADHD.

Living with ADHD can present significant challenges in daily life, but it is important to recognize that there are effective strategies and support systems available to help adults with ADHD overcome these obstacles and thrive. By gaining a deeper understanding of how ADHD impacts your daily activities and learning to implement coping mechanisms to manage symptoms, you can unlock your full potential and lead a fulfilling and successful life. It is essential to remember that you are not alone on this journey, as there are numerous resources and support networks ready to assist you in thriving with ADHD and reaching your goals. Remember to be patient with yourself as you navigate the ups and downs of living with ADHD, and don't hesitate to seek help when needed. With dedication, perseverance, and the right support, you can empower yourself to embrace your unique strengths and talents, and ultimately achieve your dreams and aspirations despite the challenges posed by ADHD.

The journey may be tough at times, but with the right mindset and tools at your disposal, you can rise above and thrive in all aspects of your life.

Chapter 2: Recognizing Your Strengths and Weaknesses

Identifying your strengths as an adult with ADHD

Recognizing and embracing your strengths as an adult with ADHD is not only important for overcoming challenges, but also for tapping into your full potential and flourishing in various aspects of your life. Despite the obstacles that may come with ADHD, there are inherent strengths that can be used to your advantage. By acknowledging and embracing these strengths, you have the opportunity to unlock your full potential and experience success in both your personal and professional endeavors. It is through this self-awareness and acceptance that you can truly thrive and make the most of your unique abilities. One of the key strengths often associated with ADHD is creativity. Many adults with ADHD possess a creative and innovative mindset that allows them to think outside the box and come up with unique solutions to problems. This creativity can be a valuable asset in a variety of fields, from art and design to business and technology. By tapping into your creative side, you can find new ways to approach challenges and excel in your chosen endeavors.

Another strength commonly found in adults with ADHD is hyperfocus. While it can be challenging to maintain focus on mundane tasks, individuals with ADHD often have the ability to hyperfocus on activities that capture their interest. This intense focus can lead to increased productivity and exceptional performance in areas where you are passionate and engaged. By identifying the activities that trigger your hyperfocus, you can leverage this strength to achieve your goals and excel in your pursuits. It is important to recognize the value of hyperfocus and use it as a tool to channel your energy and creativity towards accomplishing your objectives. Embracing your hyperfocus can empower you to make significant strides in your personal and professional endeavors, allowing you to fully capitalize on your unique strengths and abilities. Individuals with ADHD also tend to be highly energetic and enthusiastic, traits that can be advantageous in many settings.

This boundless energy can be channeled into pursuing your passions and tackling projects with vigor and determination. By harnessing your energy and enthusiasm, you can make significant progress towards your goals and inspire others with your drive and commitment.

Moreover, it is worth noting that adults with ADHD also tend to exhibit a remarkable capacity for thinking quickly and adjusting rapidly to unexpected changes. This inherent flexibility and ability to adapt can prove to be incredibly advantageous in the current fast-paced society, where the skill of being able to pivot and acclimate is crucial for achieving success. By fully embracing and harnessing your aptitude for quick thinking and adeptness at handling novel situations, you will be able to effortlessly navigate through obstacles and flourish in any given environment. In conclusion, identifying and embracing your strengths as an adult with ADHD is essential for unlocking your full potential and thriving in all aspects of your life. By recognizing your creativity, hyperfocus, energy, enthusiasm, and adaptability, you can leverage these strengths to achieve success and make a positive impact on the world around you. With the right mindset and approach, you can turn your ADHD into a superpower and thrive in all areas of your life.

It is crucial to remember that your unique perspective and abilities can contribute greatly to your personal growth and success. Embracing your strengths and utilizing them effectively can lead to increased confidence, resilience, and fulfillment in both your personal and professional endeavors.

By acknowledging and harnessing your strengths, you can enhance your relationships, excel in your career, and make a meaningful difference in the world. Remember, your ADHD is not a limitation but a powerful asset that can propel you towards achieving your goals and living a fulfilling life.

Understanding your weaknesses and how to manage them

Recognizing and understanding your weaknesses is a fundamental step in successfully navigating life with ADHD as an adult. It's essential to realize that everyone has areas where they struggle, and having ADHD can amplify these difficulties. By actively acknowledging and confronting your weaknesses, you can begin to cultivate effective strategies to not only overcome them but also tap into your innate strengths, ultimately unleashing your true capabilities and reaching your full potential. One of the first steps in understanding your weaknesses is to identify them. Take some time to reflect on areas of your life where you may struggle or feel overwhelmed. Whether it's difficulty with time management, organization, impulsivity, or emotional regulation, pinpointing your weaknesses is the first step towards finding solutions. Keep a journal or make a list of situations where you feel your ADHD symptoms are hindering your success.

Once you have identified your weaknesses, it is absolutely crucial to take proactive steps to address them and ensure they do not hinder your progress. Developing effective strategies to manage these weaknesses is key to your personal growth and success. This may involve seeking professional support from a therapist, coach, or joining a support group specifically tailored for adults with ADHD. These experts can provide invaluable guidance, personalized strategies, and practical tools to help you navigate your challenges and develop effective coping mechanisms that will serve you well in all areas of your life.

In addition to seeking professional help, you can also explore utilizing technology and organizational tools to enhance your productivity and time management skills. Incorporating these tools into your daily routine can provide structure, reminders, and assistance in staying on track with your goals. By combining professional support with technological aids, you can create a comprehensive approach to managing your weaknesses and maximizing your potential. Another key aspect of managing your weaknesses is practicing self-compassion. It's easy to be hard on yourself when you feel like your ADHD symptoms are holding you back. Remember that having ADHD is not a character flaw, but a neurological condition that presents unique challenges. Be kind to yourself and celebrate your successes, no matter how small they may seem. By practicing self-compassion, you can cultivate a positive mindset and approach your weaknesses with a growth mindset.

In conclusion, understanding your weaknesses and how to manage them is essential for thriving with ADHD as an adult. By identifying your weaknesses, seeking support, developing strategies, and practicing self-compassion, you can overcome your challenges and unlock your full potential. Remember that you are not alone in this journey, and there are resources and tools available to help you succeed. Embrace your strengths, learn from your weaknesses, and continue to strive towards your goals with confidence and determination. It is important to acknowledge that progress takes time and effort, so be patient with yourself as you navigate the ups and downs of managing ADHD. Stay connected with a supportive community, engage in regular self-care practices, and celebrate your victories no matter how small they may seem. By staying focused on your growth and development, you can transform your challenges into opportunities for personal and professional success.

Keep pushing forward with resilience and determination, knowing that you have the strength and resilience to overcome any obstacles that come your way.

Embracing your unique qualities

Embracing your unique qualities is an essential aspect of thriving with ADHD as an adult. It is important to recognize that having ADHD does not define who you are as a person, but rather adds to your individuality and strengths. By embracing your unique qualities, you can learn to harness the positive aspects of ADHD and use them to your advantage in all areas of your life. Remember that your ADHD is just one part of who you are, and by accepting and understanding it, you can empower yourself to navigate challenges and leverage your strengths effectively. Embrace your differences and see them as assets that make you stand out in a world that often values conformity. Embracing your uniqueness can lead to personal growth, self-acceptance, and a greater sense of fulfillment in all aspects of your life. One of the key aspects of embracing your unique qualities is understanding that ADHD is not a limitation, but rather a different way of processing information and interacting with the world.

By accepting this difference and viewing it as a strength, you can begin to see the many ways in which ADHD can benefit you. For example, individuals with ADHD often have high levels of creativity, energy, and passion, which can be harnessed to excel in creative fields or entrepreneurial ventures.

Another crucial aspect of fully embracing your individual qualities is recognizing and celebrating your quirks and idiosyncrasies. Individuals with ADHD often possess distinctive ways of thinking and approaching problem-solving, resulting in creative and unconventional solutions. By accepting and valuing these quirks as strengths rather than shortcomings, you can unlock your true potential and excel in every aspect of your life. It is also important to surround yourself with a supportive network of friends, family, and professionals who understand and appreciate your unique qualities. By building a strong support system, you can feel more confident in yourself and your abilities and have the encouragement and guidance you need to reach your full potential.

Surrounding yourself with people who appreciate you for who you are can help you embrace your unique qualities and thrive in all areas of your life.

In conclusion, embracing your unique qualities is a crucial aspect of thriving with ADHD as an adult. It is important to not only recognize the strengths and benefits of ADHD, but also to fully embrace your quirks and idiosyncrasies. By surrounding yourself with a supportive network that understands and accepts you for who you are, you can learn to harness your full potential and excel in all areas of your life. Embracing your unique qualities is not about changing who you are, but rather about accepting and celebrating your individuality and using it to your advantage. By embracing your unique qualities, you can unlock your full potential, tap into your creativity, and thrive as an adult with ADHD. Remember, it is your unique qualities that make you stand out and shine, so embrace them wholeheartedly and watch yourself soar to new heights of success and fulfillment.

Chapter 3: Overcoming Challenges in Daily Life

Time management strategies for adults with ADHD

A

Another helpful strategy to increase productivity is to break tasks down into smaller, more manageable steps. By doing this, you can effectively maintain focus and prevent yourself from feeling stressed or overwhelmed by the magnitude of a task at hand. For instance, if you are faced with a sizable project, consider dividing it into smaller, more manageable tasks and establish specific deadlines for each component. This approach will enable you to remain organized, stay on track, and steadily make progress towards achieving your objectives. It is also important to eliminate distractions and create a conducive work environment. This may involve turning off notifications on your phone, finding a quiet place to work, or using noise-canceling headphones. By minimizing distractions, you can improve your focus and productivity, making it easier to manage your time effectively.

Lastly, always remember to show kindness and compassion towards yourself while prioritizing self-care. Dealing with the challenges of managing ADHD can be tough, so it's crucial to nurture your mental and physical health. Set aside time for activities that bring you happiness and peace, whether it's engaging in physical exercise, pursuing hobbies, or simply enjoying the company of loved ones. By dedicating yourself to self-care practices, you can enhance your overall well-being and ultimately find it easier to effectively manage your time.

Organization tips for a clutter-free life

In order to thrive with ADHD as an adult, it is important to create an organized and clutter-free environment. This can help reduce distractions and improve focus and productivity. Here are some organization tips to help you maintain a clutter-free life:

1. Start by decluttering your space. Take some time to go through your belongings and get rid of items that you no longer need or use. This can help create more physical space in your environment and make it easier to find and access the things you need.

2. Develop a system for organizing your belongings. This could include using labels, bins, or storage containers to keep items organized and easily accessible. Having a designated place for everything can help reduce clutter and make it easier to maintain a tidy space.

3. Create a daily or weekly cleaning routine. Set aside time each day or week to clean and organize your space. This can help prevent clutter from building up and becoming overwhelming. It can also help you stay on top of tasks and maintain a sense of control over your environment.

4. Utilize technology to help you stay organized. There are many apps and tools available that can help you keep track of appointments, tasks, and deadlines. Consider using a digital calendar, to-do list, or task management app to help you stay organized and on top of your responsibilities.

5. Practice mindfulness and self-awareness. Pay attention to how clutter affects your mood and productivity. Notice when clutter starts to build up and take steps to address it before it becomes overwhelming. By being mindful of your environment and how it impacts you, you can create a space that supports your well-being and helps you thrive with ADHD.

Coping with distractions and staying focused

One of the most significant obstacles that adults with ADHD face is the constant struggle of dealing with distractions and maintaining their focus. It can be extremely exasperating to feel like your attention is being constantly tugged in various directions, hindering your ability to accomplish tasks and achieve your objectives. Despite the challenges, there are numerous effective strategies available to assist individuals in effectively managing distractions and enhancing their capacity to stay concentrated and on track towards their desired outcomes. One key strategy for coping with distractions is to create a structured environment that minimizes potential disruptions. This can include setting up a designated workspace that is free from clutter and noise, using organizational tools such as calendars and to-do lists to keep track of tasks, and establishing a routine that helps you stay on track. By creating a structured environment, you can reduce the likelihood of distractions derailing your focus.

Another helpful strategy for staying focused is to break tasks down into smaller, more manageable steps. This can help prevent feeling overwhelmed and make it easier to stay on track. By breaking tasks down into smaller steps, you can also set achievable goals for yourself, prioritize your tasks effectively, and track your progress more effectively. This can help you stay motivated and focused on completing tasks, leading to a greater sense of accomplishment and productivity in your work. It's also important to recognize when distractions are starting to pull you away from your work and take steps to refocus your attention. This might involve taking a short break, practicing mindfulness techniques, or using strategies such as the Pomodoro technique to work in short bursts with frequent breaks. By being proactive about managing distractions, you can improve your ability to stay focused and productive.

Finally, it's crucial to constantly remind yourself that managing distractions and maintaining focus is a continuous journey. Setbacks and instances of losing focus are completely normal, but it's vital to show compassion towards yourself and persist in your efforts to enhance your concentration. Through the utilization of these strategies and the cultivation of additional coping mechanisms, you can gradually master the art of thriving with ADHD and ultimately unlock your true potential as an adult.

Chapter 4: Building Healthy Habits for Success

Establishing a daily routine that works for you

stablishing a daily routine that works for you is crucial for adults with ADHD in order to thrive and reach their full potential. Living with ADHD can present unique challenges when it comes to staying organized and managing time effectively. However, by creating a structured daily routine, individuals with ADHD can better manage their symptoms and improve their overall quality of life. It is important to prioritize tasks, set realistic goals, and incorporate breaks and self-care activities throughout the day to maintain focus and energy levels. Additionally, seeking support from healthcare professionals, therapists, or support groups can provide valuable resources and strategies for managing ADHD symptoms and navigating daily challenges. By consistently following a personalized routine and utilizing available resources, individuals with ADHD can cultivate a sense of control, productivity, and fulfillment in their daily lives. One key tip for establishing a daily routine that works for you is to start by identifying your most important tasks and priorities

.

By focusing on what needs to be done first, you can better allocate your time and energy to the tasks that matter most. This can help prevent feelings of overwhelm and ensure that you are making progress on your goals each day.

Creating a successful daily routine involves more than just following a strict schedule – it also requires prioritizing regular breaks and self-care. For adults with ADHD, maintaining focus for extended periods can be challenging, making it crucial to incorporate opportunities for rest and rejuvenation throughout the day. By taking these breaks, you can boost your productivity levels, avoid burnout, and sustain your motivation and engagement in your daily responsibilities. In addition to breaks, it's also helpful to establish a consistent sleep schedule and prioritize getting enough rest each night. Adequate sleep is essential for managing ADHD symptoms and improving overall cognitive function. By making sleep a priority in your daily routine, you can enhance your focus, concentration, and mood, ultimately setting yourself up for success in all areas of your life.

Establishing a daily routine that works for you as an adult with ADHD is a journey that requires patience, self-awareness, and flexibility. It may take time and effort to strike the right balance of tasks, breaks, and self-care activities that cater to your individual needs and preferences. However, by staying persistent and dedicated, you have the power to create a routine that not only supports you but also helps you flourish. It's important to remember to show yourself kindness and compassion throughout this process, and to take pride in even the smallest victories as you continue to unlock your full potential and live your best life.

The importance of exercise and nutrition for ADHD management

In order to effectively manage ADHD symptoms, it is imperative for adults with ADHD to prioritize exercise, nutrition, and self-care practices. The importance of maintaining a healthy lifestyle cannot be overstated when it comes to managing the challenges that come with ADHD. Incorporating regular exercise, a balanced diet, mindfulness techniques, adequate sleep, and stress management strategies into your daily routine can have a significant impact on your overall well-being and ability to thrive with ADHD. Taking care of your physical, mental, and emotional health is key to managing ADHD symptoms and improving your quality of life. Exercise has been shown to have a positive effect on ADHD symptoms by increasing dopamine and norepinephrine levels in the brain. These neurotransmitters play a key role in regulating attention, focus, and impulse control, which are often areas of difficulty for individuals with ADHD.

Engaging in physical activity can help improve cognitive function, reduce hyperactivity, and enhance mood, making it an essential component of ADHD management.

In addition to exercise, nutrition also plays a crucial role in managing ADHD symptoms. A diet rich in fruits, vegetables, whole grains, and lean proteins can provide the essential nutrients needed for optimal brain function. Avoiding processed foods, sugary snacks, and caffeine can help stabilize energy levels and improve focus. Making healthy food choices can also help regulate mood and decrease impulsivity, making it easier to stay on track with daily tasks and responsibilities.

By prioritizing exercise and nutrition, adults with ADHD can take control of their symptoms and improve their overall quality of life. Establishing a consistent exercise routine and creating a meal plan that supports brain health can make a significant difference in managing ADHD symptoms. It is important to remember that managing ADHD is a multifaceted approach, and incorporating lifestyle changes such as exercise and nutrition can complement other strategies such as medication and therapy.

In conclusion, exercise and nutrition are essential components of ADHD management for adults looking to thrive with ADHD. By making healthy lifestyle choices, individuals can improve their cognitive function, regulate their mood, and enhance their overall well-being. It is never too late to prioritize your health and well-being, and taking steps to incorporate exercise and nutrition into your daily routine can have a profound impact on your ability to thrive with ADHD. Remember, consistency is key when it comes to maintaining a healthy lifestyle. It's important to set realistic goals and make gradual changes to your diet and exercise routine. By staying committed to your health and well-being, you can experience long-term benefits that will positively impact your life in numerous ways. So, don't hesitate to start making positive changes today for a healthier, happier future!

Developing coping mechanisms for stress and anxiety

Living with ADHD as an adult can come with its own set of challenges, one of the most common being stress and anxiety. It's important to recognize that these feelings are normal and valid, but it's also crucial to develop coping mechanisms to help navigate through these difficult moments. In this subchapter, we will explore some effective strategies for managing stress and anxiety, allowing you to thrive despite the obstacles that ADHD may present. It's essential to remember that self-care plays a crucial role in managing these challenges, so taking time for relaxation and mindfulness practices can greatly benefit your mental well-being. Additionally, seeking support from a therapist or support group can provide valuable tools and resources for coping with the daily struggles that may arise. Remember, it's okay to not be okay sometimes, but with the right strategies and support, you can overcome the obstacles that ADHD presents and live a fulfilling life. One powerful coping mechanism for stress and anxiety is mindfulness meditation.

By practicing mindfulness, you can learn to stay present in the moment and observe your thoughts and feelings without judgment. This can help you become more aware of your triggers for stress and anxiety, allowing you to address them more effectively.

Incorporating mindfulness meditation into your daily routine can provide a sense of calm and clarity, making it easier to navigate through challenging situations.

Another helpful strategy for managing stress and anxiety is exercise. Physical activity has been shown to reduce levels of cortisol, the stress hormone, and release endorphins, the body's natural mood lifters. Whether it's going for a run, practicing yoga, or taking a dance class, finding a form of exercise that you enjoy can be a great way to relieve stress and anxiety. Plus, regular exercise can improve your overall well-being and help you feel more resilient in the face of adversity.

In addition to mindfulness, meditation and exercise, it's important to prioritize self-care as a way to cope with stress and anxiety. This can include activities such as getting enough sleep, eating a balanced diet, and engaging in hobbies that bring you joy. Taking care of yourself physically and emotionally can help you build resilience and better cope with the challenges that come with living with ADHD. Remember that self-care is not selfish – it's essential for your overall well-being.

Lastly, seeking support from others can be invaluable in managing stress and anxiety. Whether it's talking to a therapist, joining a support group, or confiding in a trusted friend or family member, sharing your feelings and experiences with others can provide comfort and perspective. Knowing that you're not alone in your struggles can be a powerful reminder that there is hope and help available. By developing coping mechanisms for stress and anxiety and seeking support when needed, you can thrive as an adult with ADHD and unlock your full potential. It's important to remember that reaching out for help is a sign of strength, not weakness. Building a strong support network can help you navigate the challenges of ADHD with greater resilience and confidence. Additionally, exploring different forms of therapy and self-care practices can empower you to better manage your symptoms and improve your overall well-being.

Remember, you don't have to face ADHD alone - there are resources and people who are ready to help you on your journey towards a fulfilling and successful life.

Chapter 5: Navigating Relationships and Communication

Communicating effectively with loved ones about your ADHD

In the decades following my graduation, ADHD played a significant role in my professional life. Deadlines, multitasking, and the fast pace of the work environment seemed daunting. Creating an open channel of communication with my superiors, utilizing the skills I'd developed, and applying the coping mechanisms I'd learned allowed me to create a supportive work environment that has sustained me through years in my profession. With ongoing effort, I was able to achieve professional growth and satisfaction. Life with ADHD can present real difficulties. Being easily sidetracked, struggling to focus, and always feeling two steps behind with the latest requests from those around you can be tough. Yet, it has been an opportunity to push myself, to find my voice in a world where lacking it is a real barrier to success.

Talking about the issues I need help with and developing a "bag of tricks" for working around difficulties have been essential strategies. Effectively communicating with loved ones about your ADHD is a crucial aspect of successfully navigating life with this condition as an adult.

it is vital to keep in mind that ADHD is a neurodevelopmental disorder that impacts your capacity to concentrate, plan, and efficiently manage time.By openly discussing your ADHD with your loved ones, you can provide them with insight into your struggles and enlist their support in effectively managing them. This open dialogue can strengthen your relationships and create a supportive network to help you thrive despite the challenges posed by ADHD. When talking to your loved ones about your ADHD, it's important to approach the conversation with honesty and openness. Be prepared to explain what ADHD is, how it affects you on a daily basis, and what strategies you use to cope with its symptoms. You may also want to share any specific ways in which your loved ones can support you, such as helping you stay organized or reminding you of important tasks.

It's also important to listen to your loved ones' perspectives and concerns about your ADHD. They may have questions or misunderstandings about the condition, and it's important to address these in a compassionate and patient manner. By opening a dialogue about your ADHD, you can strengthen your relationships and create a supportive environment for yourself.

In addition to talking to your loved ones about your ADHD, it can also be helpful to involve them in your treatment plan. This may include attending therapy sessions together, engaging in family counseling, or simply keeping them informed about your progress in managing your symptoms. By involving your loved ones in your treatment, you can create a united front against ADHD and work together towards positive outcomes.

Overall, communicating effectively with loved ones about your ADHD is a crucial step in thriving as an adult with this condition. By being open, honest, and proactive in your discussions, you can create a supportive network of understanding and empathy that will help you navigate the challenges of ADHD with strength and resilience. Remember that you are not alone in this journey, and that your loved ones can be valuable allies in your quest to unlock your full potential.

It is important to maintain regular communication with your support system, as their understanding and encouragement can make a significant difference in your daily life. By sharing your struggles and triumphs with those closest to you, you can build a strong foundation of trust and support that will empower you to face any obstacles that come your way. Together, you can work towards a brighter future filled with growth, resilience, and personal fulfillment.

Building strong relationships and support systems

Developing strong relationships and support systems is absolutely essential for adults with ADHD to not only survive but also thrive in their day-to-day existence. While ADHD can pose distinctive obstacles in the realm of maintaining connections, having the appropriate resources and perspective can enable individuals to establish deep and meaningful bonds that offer the necessary assistance for triumph. This section will delve into various tactics for constructing robust relationships and support systems that are instrumental in assisting those with ADHD in effectively managing the constant ebbs and flows of their daily routines. One of the first steps in building strong relationships and support systems is to communicate openly and honestly with those around you. It is important to educate your friends, family, and colleagues about ADHD and how it impacts your life.

By being transparent about your struggles and strengths, you can create a supportive environment where others can better understand and empathize with your experiences.

Another crucial aspect of cultivating strong and meaningful relationships is ensuring that you are surrounded by individuals who not only uplift and encourage you, but also truly understand and support you through the challenges of living with ADHD. It is essential to seek out friends and mentors who exhibit qualities such as positivity, patience, and empathy, as they can offer valuable emotional support and guidance when you are facing difficult moments. By surrounding yourself with such individuals, you are more likely to stay motivated, focused, and determined to reach your goals, despite the obstacles that may come your way. In addition to fostering personal relationships, it is also important to build a support system that includes professionals who specialize in ADHD. This may include therapists, coaches, or doctors who can provide tailored strategies and interventions to help you manage your symptoms effectively.

Seeking professional help can empower you to develop coping mechanisms and skills that will enable you to thrive in all areas of your life.

Lastly, do not overlook the importance of self-care when it comes to developing strong relationships and support networks. It is crucial to prioritize your physical, emotional, and mental well-being in order to nurture positive connections with those around you. Make sure to dedicate time to activities that bring you happiness and relaxation, whether it be through exercise, mindfulness practices, or engaging in hobbies that help you de-stress. By focusing on self-care and investing in your own growth, you will be able to cultivate the resilience and inner strength necessary to navigate the challenges of living with ADHD and establish meaningful relationships that will serve as a source of support and encouragement on your journey towards personal growth and fulfillment.

Managing conflicts and misunderstandings

Conflict and misunderstandings are a natural part of human relationships, but for adults with ADHD, they can sometimes feel overwhelming. In this subchapter, we will explore strategies for managing conflicts and misunderstandings in a way that allows you to thrive with ADHD. By learning how to navigate these challenges effectively, you can strengthen your relationships and improve your overall well-being. It is important to remember that communication is key in resolving conflicts, and practicing active listening can help in understanding others' perspectives. Additionally, setting boundaries and expressing your needs assertively can prevent misunderstandings and promote healthier interactions. By incorporating these strategies into your daily life, you can cultivate more harmonious relationships and navigate the complexities of ADHD with resilience and grace. One of the first steps in managing conflicts and misunderstandings is to recognize when they are occurring.

For adults with ADHD, it can be easy to overlook or misinterpret social cues, leading to misunderstandings that can escalate into conflicts. By being aware of your own tendencies and triggers, you can begin to address these issues before they spiral out of control.

Effective communication is vital in addressing conflicts and avoiding misunderstandings. For individuals with ADHD, verbal communication can pose challenges and hinder the ability to articulate thoughts and emotions effectively. To enhance communication skills, it is beneficial to actively listen, seek clarification through questions, and welcome feedback from others. By honing these strategies, you can enhance your ability to communicate clearly and minimize the potential for misunderstandings to occur. It is also important to take a step back and consider the other person's perspective during conflicts. Adults with ADHD can sometimes be so focused on their own thoughts and feelings that they neglect to consider how their words and actions are affecting others. By practicing empathy and putting yourself in the other person's shoes, you can gain a deeper understanding of their point of view and work towards a resolution that benefits both parties.

Finally, it is essential to actively engage in the process of learning from each conflict and misunderstanding that arises. Rather than simply brushing these challenges aside as failures, it is crucial to recognize them as invaluable opportunities for personal growth and self-improvement. By taking the time to reflect on what went wrong, pinpointing strategies that proved effective, and implementing necessary adjustments for the future, you could cultivate and enhance your conflict resolution skills significantly. In doing so, you will not only foster healthier relationships in all aspects of your life, but also develop a deeper understanding of yourself and your interactions with others.

Chapter 6: Thriving in the Workplace

Advocating for accommodations in the workplace

As a child, I was always perceived as daydreaming or just not paying attention during class. The consensus from my family, teachers, and friends was that I was lazy, uninterested, or simply not trying hard enough. It wasn't until I was a teenager that I was diagnosed with Attention-Deficit/Hyperactivity Disorder (ADHD) and given an explanation for the difficulties I had experienced when I was younger. However, a diagnosis didn't make it any easier to live with ADHD. ADHD symptoms vary from person to person, but my problems with focus were both hyperactive and inattentive in nature. This meant that I was equally inept at sitting still and completing a task as I was at switching to a new project at the expense of the current one in its early stages. Everyday chores, from cleaning my room to completing homework assignments, were unmanageably long and seemingly endless. Yet, there were also unexpected benefits. I discovered that the quicksilver quality of my mind made me a natural at occupations requiring lateral thinking.

In the workplace, adults with ADHD may face challenges that their neurotypical colleagues do not.

From struggling to stay focused during long meetings to feeling overwhelmed by deadlines, navigating a traditional work environment can be particularly challenging for individuals with ADHD. It is important for employers to recognize the unique needs of employees with ADHD and work towards creating a more accommodating and understanding work environment. By providing necessary accommodations and support, employers can help level the playing field and promote inclusivity in the workplace for those with ADHD. Advocating for accommodations not only benefits individuals with ADHD, but also contributes to a more positive and productive work environment for all employees. Employers should also consider implementing flexible work schedules, providing additional training on coping strategies for ADHD, and fostering open communication channels to ensure that employees with ADHD feel supported and valued in the workplace.

Additionally, offering resources such as coaching or counseling services can further assist individuals with ADHD in managing their symptoms and improving their performance at work.

Ultimately, creating a work culture that embraces diversity and accommodates different neurodivergent needs will lead to a more inclusive and successful work environment for everyone involved.

One crucial step in advocating for accommodation in the workplace is to have an open, transparent, and candid conversation with your employer or HR department regarding your ADHD. By openly sharing your diagnosis and discussing how it affects your work performance, you can collaborate to pinpoint potential accommodations that can enhance your productivity and overall well-being in your position. This could involve implementing measures such as flexible work hours, providing noise-canceling headphones, or granting access to a peaceful and conducive workspace where you can thrive and excel.

It's crucial to keep in mind that advocating for accommodation in the workplace is not about seeking preferential treatment or providing justifications for your ADHD. Rather, it involves acknowledging your individual needs and collaborating with your employer to identify effective solutions that enable you to excel. By presenting your request for accommodation in a constructive and forward-thinking manner, you can effectively communicate to your employer the advantages that these adjustments can offer both you and the overall organization, fostering a more inclusive and supportive work environment.

In addition to having a conversation with your employer, it can also be helpful to educate yourself about your rights as an individual with ADHD in the workplace. Understanding the Americans with Disabilities Act (ADA) and other relevant laws can help you advocate for the accommodations you need with confidence and clarity. By arming yourself with knowledge and understanding your rights, you can approach conversations about accommodations from a place of empowerment. Taking the time to research and familiarize yourself with the specific protections and resources available to you as a person with ADHD can further strengthen your ability to effectively communicate your needs and ensure that you are receiving the support necessary for your success in the workplace.

Ultimately, advocating for accommodations in the workplace is about creating a more inclusive and supportive environment for individuals with ADHD. By working collaboratively with your employer to identify and implement accommodations that align with your specific needs and challenges, you can unlock your full potential and thrive in your chosen career path. Remember, you are not alone in this journey – there is a wealth of resources and support available to assist you in navigating the unique challenges of ADHD in the workplace and unlocking your true potential.
It is crucial to maintain open and proactive communication with your employer regarding your needs, as well as to educate yourself about your rights and the various accommodations that are available to you. Seeking out mentorship and building connections with other individuals who share similar experiences with ADHD can provide invaluable support and guidance as you navigate the ups and downs of your professional journey.

Do not hesitate to reach out for help and make use of the resources at your disposal – you deserve to not only succeed but also to thrive in your workplace environment.

Strategies for staying organized and productive at work

Staying organized and productive at work can be a significant challenge for adults with ADHD, but with the right strategies in place, it is absolutely possible to not just survive, but thrive in a work environment. One key strategy that has proven to be effective is creating a detailed daily to-do list. This list should outline all the tasks that need to be completed for the day, prioritizing them from most important to least important. By breaking down tasks into smaller, manageable chunks, individuals with ADHD can more easily stay focused and on track throughout the day, leading to increased productivity and overall success in the workplace.

Another helpful strategy is to utilize tools and technology to stay organized. In today's digital age, there is a wide array of apps and software programs specifically designed to assist individuals with ADHD in managing their time effectively. These tools can help keep track of important deadlines, appointments, and daily tasks, ultimately leading to increased productivity and efficiency in the workplace. From intuitive calendar apps to comprehensive task management tools, finding the right technology that suits your needs and preferences can significantly enhance your ability to stay organized and focused on your responsibilities. Creating specific routines and rituals can greatly benefit adults with ADHD by providing structure and stability in their daily lives. Additionally, incorporating mindfulness practices and relaxation techniques into your daily routine can also help in managing symptoms of ADHD. Taking breaks, practicing deep breathing exercises, and engaging in physical activity can all contribute to reducing stress and improving focus.

It's important to experiment with different strategies and techniques to find what works best for you and to be open to adjusting your routines as needed to optimize your productivity and overall well-being.

In addition to establishing a consistent morning routine, individuals can also incorporate mindfulness practices, such as meditation or journaling, to start their day on a positive note. Furthermore, incorporating rituals for breaks throughout the day, such as taking short walks or practicing deep breathing exercises, can help improve focus and productivity. By implementing these strategies, individuals with ADHD can better manage their symptoms and enhance their overall well-being. It is essential for adults with ADHD to prioritize creating a clutter-free work environment to minimize distractions and increase productivity. Clutter has the potential to cause feelings of overwhelm and hinder focus, making it challenging to stay on task and accomplish goals. Additionally, setting boundaries with technology use and scheduling regular breaks for physical activity can also be beneficial in maintaining focus and reducing impulsivity.

Engaging in activities that promote relaxation and self-care, such as yoga or spending time in nature, can further support individuals with ADHD in managing their symptoms and maintaining a balanced lifestyle.

By dedicating time to decluttering your workspace, whether it be a physical desk or a digital desktop, you can significantly improve organization and efficiency within your work environment, ultimately leading to a more productive and successful workday. In addition, creating a system for organizing documents and tasks, such as color-coding or labeling, can further enhance your productivity and reduce feelings of overwhelm. Lastly, it's crucial for adults with ADHD to prioritize self-care and mental health. Taking breaks throughout the day, engaging in regular exercise, and incorporating mindfulness or meditation practices into your routine can significantly reduce stress levels and enhance focus and productivity. By dedicating time to these strategies, you can unlock your full potential and thrive in the workplace as an adult with ADHD, ultimately leading to a more fulfilling and balanced life.

Remember to also prioritize getting enough sleep, maintaining a healthy diet, and seeking support from mental health professionals when needed.

Your well-being is essential for your success in both your personal and professional life.

Balancing work and self-care

Balancing work and self-care can be particularly challenging for adults with ADHD, as the demands of daily life can frequently feel insurmountable and exhausting. However, it is essential to find a harmonious equilibrium between work responsibilities and prioritizing self-care to effectively manage ADHD symptoms and flourish in various aspects of your life. Throughout this upcoming subchapter, we will delve into a plethora of strategies and practical tips aimed at assisting you in not only meeting your work obligations but also emphasizing the importance of self-care and overall well-being. One key tip for balancing work and self-care is to establish a daily routine that includes time for both work tasks and self-care activities. This can help create a sense of structure and predictability in your day, which can be especially helpful for individuals with ADHD. Set aside specific blocks of time for work tasks, breaks, and self-care activities such as exercise, mindfulness practices, or hobbies that bring you joy.

Another crucial aspect of finding balance between work and self-care is establishing clear boundaries with your time and energy. It is essential to recognize when you need to say no to extra work responsibilities or obligations that may lead to burnout and hinder your self-care practices. By prioritizing tasks according to their significance and immediacy, you can effectively manage your workload and avoid unnecessary stress. Don't hesitate to seek assistance or delegate tasks when necessary. Always remember that taking care of yourself is not a selfish act, but a vital component of maintaining your overall well-being and productivity. In addition to setting boundaries, practicing self-compassion is essential for adults with ADHD who are trying to balance work and self-care. Be gentle with yourself when you make mistakes or struggle to stay on top of your responsibilities. Remember that ADHD is a neurodevelopmental disorder that can make certain tasks more challenging, and it is okay to ask for support or accommodations when needed.

Treat yourself with kindness and understanding as you navigate the demands of everyday life.

Finally, finding ways to incorporate self-care into your workday can help you maintain a sense of balance and well-being. Take short breaks throughout the day to stretch, walk, or engage in a quick mindfulness exercise. Practice good self-care habits such as staying hydrated, eating nutritious foods, and getting enough sleep. Prioritize activities that help you recharge and relax, such as spending time outdoors, connecting with loved ones, or engaging in creative pursuits. By making self-care a priority in your daily routine, you can better manage your ADHD symptoms and thrive in both your work and personal life. Remember to listen to your body and mind and give yourself permission to take time for self-care even during a busy day. Consider incorporating relaxation techniques like deep breathing exercises, meditation, or yoga into your routine to help reduce stress and improve your overall well-being. Don't forget to set boundaries and learn to say no when necessary to avoid burnout and overwhelm.

Ultimately, prioritizing self-care is essential for maintaining a healthy balance in your life and ensuring long-term success in managing your ADHD symptoms.

Chapter 7: Embracing Your Potential

Setting goals and working towards them

Setting goals and working towards them is a crucial aspect of thriving with ADHD as an adult. Many individuals with ADHD may struggle with setting and achieving goals due to challenges with focus, organization, and time management. It is important to understand that these obstacles can be overcome with the right strategies in place, such as breaking down goals into smaller, manageable tasks and creating a structured routine that supports goal achievement. By developing a growth mindset and seeking support from professionals or peers, individuals with ADHD can make significant progress towards their goals and ultimately thrive in their personal and professional lives. One key strategy for setting goals and working towards them is breaking them down into smaller, more manageable tasks. This can help to prevent feeling overwhelmed and increase the likelihood of success. By creating a step-by-step plan, you can stay focused and on track, even when faced with distractions or setbacks.

For example, if your goal is to start a new exercise routine, break it down into smaller tasks such as researching workout options, scheduling time for exercise, and gradually increasing your activity level.

Another crucial aspect of setting goals and working towards them is maintaining a high level of organization. This entails utilizing various tools such as digital calendars, detailed to-do lists, and timely reminders to effectively monitor your progress and ensure that you meet deadlines. By establishing a consistent routine and cultivating a structured environment, you can effectively eliminate potential distractions and significantly enhance your overall productivity. Moreover, seeking encouragement and assistance from supportive friends, family members, or a professional therapist can offer valuable accountability and motivation, ultimately aiding you in maintaining focus and determination towards achieving your goals. It is also important to be flexible and adaptable when working towards your goals. Life is unpredictable, and unexpected challenges may arise that can derail your progress. By remaining open to change and willing to adjust your plans as needed, you can navigate obstacles more effectively and continue moving forward.

Remember that setbacks are a natural part of the goal-setting process, and it is essential to learn from them and keep pushing towards your ultimate objectives.

In conclusion, setting specific and achievable goals and consistently working towards them is a crucial and effective strategy for individuals living with ADHD as adults. By breaking down larger goals into smaller, manageable tasks, staying organized, seeking support from loved ones or professionals, and maintaining a flexible mindset, you can effectively navigate obstacles and ultimately achieve success in various aspects of your life. It is important to remember that progress is a gradual process that requires dedication and effort, but with unwavering determination and perseverance, you can unlock your full potential and thrive in all areas of your personal and professional life. Remember that setbacks are a natural part of the journey, and it's essential to practice self-compassion and patience as you work towards your goals. Embrace the process of growth and learning, and celebrate even the smallest victories along the way. Each step forward, no matter how small, is a testament to your strength and resilience.

As you continue on your path towards success, remember to prioritize self-care and mental well-being, as these are essential components of maintaining balance and sustainable progress.

By embracing a growth mindset and facing challenges with courage and determination, you can overcome any obstacles that come your way and achieve your dreams.

Celebrating your successes and learning from setbacks

Celebrating your successes is an important aspect of thriving with ADHD as an adult. Oftentimes, individuals with ADHD can be hyper-focused on their setbacks and struggles, leading them to overlook their achievements. By taking the time to acknowledge and celebrate your successes, no matter how small they may seem, you are reinforcing positive behaviors and boosting your self-confidence. This can help you stay motivated and continue making progress towards your goals. Whether it's completing a task on time, getting positive feedback at work, or simply remembering to take your medication, be sure to take a moment to pat yourself on the back and recognize your accomplishments. Remember that every step forward, no matter how small, is a step in the right direction towards a more fulfilling and successful life. Embrace your victories, no matter how insignificant they may seem, as they all contribute to your growth and progress.

So, celebrate your wins and use them as fuel to keep pushing forward on your journey towards personal and professional fulfillment.

On the flip side, setbacks are inevitable when living with ADHD. However, it's important to view setbacks as learning opportunities rather than failures. When faced with a setback, take a step back and evaluate what went wrong. Was it a lack of organization, poor time management, or simply a slip-up? By identifying the root cause of the setback, you can develop strategies to prevent it from happening again in the future. Remember, setbacks are not a reflection of your abilities or worth as an individual. They are simply temporary roadblocks that can be overcome with the right mindset and tools.

One way to effectively learn from setbacks is to keep a journal or log of your experiences. By documenting your successes and setbacks, you can track patterns and identify triggers that may be contributing to your challenges. This can help you develop a better understanding of your ADHD symptoms and how they impact your daily life. Additionally, journaling can serve as a valuable tool for reflection and growth, as you can look back on past entries to see how far you've come and what areas still need improvement.

Another crucial aspect of celebrating successes and learning from setbacks is the importance of seeking support from others. Having a strong support system in place, whether it be friends, family, or a therapist, can greatly enhance your ability to process your experiences and navigate the challenges of living with ADHD. These individuals can offer a unique perspective, valuable insights, and practical advice to help you effectively manage your symptoms. In addition to seeking support from those close to you, consider joining a support group or online community specifically for individuals with ADHD. Connecting with others who share similar experiences can provide a sense of belonging and comfort, knowing that you are not alone in your struggles. By surrounding yourself with a supportive network of people, you can strengthen your resilience and find the encouragement you need to thrive despite the obstacles you may face.

In conclusion, celebrating your successes and learning from setbacks are essential components of thriving with ADHD as an adult. By taking the time to acknowledge your achievements, reflect on your setbacks, and seek support from others, you can develop the resilience and self-awareness needed to overcome the challenges associated with ADHD. Remember, you can achieve great things, and with the right mindset and tools, you can unlock your full potential and thrive in all areas of your life. It is important to embrace the journey of personal growth and continue to cultivate a positive mindset. By recognizing the progress, you have made and remaining open to learning from your experiences, you can continue to build upon your strengths and overcome any obstacles that may come your way. With perseverance and a growth mindset, you can navigate the complexities of living with ADHD and flourish in all aspects of your life.

Finding fulfillment and happiness as an adult with ADHD

Living with ADHD as an adult can present unique challenges, but it is possible to find fulfillment and happiness despite the obstacles. In this subchapter, we will explore strategies and tips for thriving with ADHD and living a fulfilling life. By understanding your strengths and weaknesses, setting realistic goals, and developing coping mechanisms, you can unlock your potential, overcome setbacks, and thrive as an adult with ADHD. It's important to remember that self-compassion and seeking support from loved ones and professionals can also play a crucial role in your journey towards a fulfilling and successful life with ADHD. One of the first steps to finding fulfillment and happiness as an adult with ADHD is to embrace your unique talents and strengths. Many adults with ADHD are creative, energetic, and innovative thinkers. By focusing on your strengths and leveraging them in your daily life, you can build confidence and find success in various aspects of your life.

Whether it's pursuing a creative hobby, starting a new project at work, or engaging in physical activity, embracing your strengths can help you thrive with ADHD.

Setting realistic goals is another crucial aspect of finding fulfillment and happiness as an adult with ADHD. It is essential to recognize that it can be challenging to navigate through the daily demands of life. However, by breaking down your goals into smaller, more manageable tasks, you can make steady progress and experience a profound sense of achievement.

By setting clear, achievable goals, you are more likely to stay motivated and maintain focus, ultimately leading to a heightened sense of fulfillment in various aspects of your life. Developing coping mechanisms to manage the symptoms of ADHD is crucial for thriving as an adult with the condition. It's important to recognize that everyone's journey with ADHD is unique, and what works for one person may not work for another. Some individuals may find that establishing a strict daily routine helps them stay on track, while others may benefit from utilizing organizational tools such as planners or apps to help them stay organized.

Seeking support from a therapist or coach can also be incredibly beneficial in helping individuals develop effective coping strategies and navigate the challenges of ADHD.

By taking the time to identify your specific triggers and developing personalized coping mechanisms to address them, you can greatly improve your ability to focus, stay organized, and manage your time effectively. It's important to remember that managing

ADHD is an ongoing process, and it may take some trial and error to find the strategies that work best for you. With patience, perseverance, and a willingness to seek help when needed, you can empower yourself to lead a more fulfilling and balanced life despite the challenges of ADHD.

In conclusion, finding fulfillment and happiness as an adult with ADHD is not only possible, but achievable with the right strategies and mindset. By embracing your strengths, setting realistic goals, and consistently working on developing coping mechanisms, you can unlock your true potential and thrive with ADHD. It is important to remember that you are not alone in your journey, as there are numerous resources and support systems available to help you navigate the challenges of living with ADHD. With determination, perseverance, and a positive outlook, you can lead a fulfilling, successful, and ultimately happy life as an adult with ADHD. It's crucial to prioritize self-care, practice mindfulness, and seek professional help when needed. Building a strong support network, engaging in regular exercise, and maintaining a healthy lifestyle can also significantly impact your overall well-being and ability to manage ADHD effectively.

Remember to celebrate your accomplishments, no matter how small, and always strive for progress rather than perfection. By staying resilient, adaptable, and open to growth, you can continue to thrive and find joy in the journey of living with ADHD.

I

Conclusion: Unlocking Your Potential - Recap of key takeaways - Encouragement for embracing your potential as an adult with ADHD

In conclusion, unlocking your potential as an adult with ADHD is not only possible, but it is also crucial for living a fulfilling and successful life. Throughout this book, we have explored various strategies and techniques to help you thrive with ADHD, from managing your time effectively to harnessing your unique strengths. By embracing your potential and learning to work with your ADHD rather than against it, you can achieve great things and live a life that is truly meaningful.

 Remember, it's important to prioritize self-care, practice self-compassion, and seek support when needed. Don't be afraid to set boundaries, practice mindfulness, and celebrate your achievements, no matter how small they may seem. With determination, perseverance, and a positive mindset, you can overcome any challenges that come your way and create a life filled with purpose and fulfillment. One key takeaway from this book is the importance of self-awareness.

By taking the time to truly understand your strengths and weaknesses, you can effectively harness your unique talents and navigate through your obstacles with greater ease.

This level of self-awareness not only empowers you to establish achievable goals, but also enables you to efficiently allocate your time, cultivate positive habits, and prioritize your overall well-being for long-term success and fulfillment.

By taking the time to reflect on your own experiences and learn from them, you can unlock your full potential as an adult with ADHD.

Another crucial takeaway to consider is the incredible impact of mindset on one's success. By embracing a growth mindset and having faith in your capacity to continuously improve and evolve, you could conquer challenges and reach your aspirations. Rather than perceiving ADHD as a drawback, recognize it as a distinctive vantage point that can be utilized to spark creativity and ingenuity. Through reshaping your mindset and emphasizing your capabilities, you can unleash your full potential and flourish as an individual navigating adulthood with ADHD.

I encourage you to continue exploring and implementing the strategies and techniques discussed in this book. Remember that progress takes time and effort, so be patient with yourself as you work towards unlocking your potential. Surround yourself with supportive individuals who understand and appreciate your unique strengths, and don't be afraid to ask for help when you need it. By embracing your potential and making the most of your ADHD, you can live a fulfilling and successful life that is true to who you are.

It is important to also acknowledge that setbacks and obstacles may arise along the way, but it is how you choose to respond to them that will ultimately define your journey. Embrace challenges as opportunities for growth and learning, and remain resilient in the face of adversity. By staying committed to your personal development and staying true to your goals, you will continue to make strides towards success and fulfillment. Keep pushing yourself outside of your comfort zone and challenging yourself to reach new heights. Remember, you are capable of achieving great things and your ADHD should be seen as a unique asset that sets you apart from others. Keep believing in yourself and never underestimate the power of a positive mindset in shaping your future.

In conclusion, I want to emphasize that you are never alone on this journey. There exists a vibrant and supportive community of adults with ADHD who are actively working towards accepting their capabilities and leading fulfilling lives. By openly discussing your challenges, reaching out for assistance, and persistently expanding your knowledge and skills, you have the ability to unlock your full potential and flourish as an adult with ADHD.